Why Should I] Foods?

The Pro's, the Con's, & Everything You'd Want To Know

By
A.J. Parker

Table of Contents

Introduction

The world is changing – whether we like it or not – and more importantly what we eat is changing too. Food that our parents ate is completely different than the food we eat.

I recently heard that most of the foods options we have today are potentially harmful – that it's genetically modified and filled with pesticides, chemicals, and lack the nutrients our bodies need. Then, I heard organic food is the ONLY way to go if you want to be healthy!

To be completely honest, I didn't know anything about organic food, so I decided to go on a quest to find out what it is, what foods ARE good to eat, and why I should eat organic foods. In this process, I learned that most people DO NOT know what organic food is or WHY they should eat it. And I was on a quest to determine the truth about organic foods!

Throughout this book I'll share with you what I've learned from the advantages to the disadvantages of eating organic foods, and how organic food impacts your health. I'll also explain how eating non-organic food affects your health.

Lets get started!

Chapter 1 - Differences Between Organic And Non Organic

The major difference of organic foods from the non-organic is the way on how they are grown, produced, packed and handled. This difference will give you an overview of the expected effects of patronizing non-organic products.

o. Organic fruits and vegetables are given natural fertilizers such as manure and compost that do not destroy the natural properties of the soil. Conventional foods are grown with industrial and synthetic fertilizers that are absorbed and retained by the soil for long years.

1. In organic farming, the fertility of the soil is maintained through a process called crop rotation. Vegetables and fruits are planted according to the season that will offer varied selection all year round. Modern method solely depends on commercialized fertilizers that eliminate soil fertility. Prohibited fertilizers contain heavy metals like cadmium and mercury that are retained in the farmland and absorbed by the crops later.

2. Organic farming methods promote biodiversity by using natural methods in getting rid of pests like making traps. In the conventional way of farming, pests and plant diseases are treated with big amounts of insecticides and pesticides.

3. Organic farmers use natural weed killers such as mulch or hand weeding while conventional farming uses chemical herbicides to prevent the growth or existence of weeds, chemicals that can have an adverse effect on a person's health.

4. Organic livestock treats the animals humanely; the animals are free to walk around the pasture

and provided with clean housing to keep them from diseases. They are raised on an all-grass diet and are not given unnatural appetite enhancers. Vaccinations and giving supplements are not allowed. Modern farming depends mostly on antibiotics, growth hormones and some medications that include too many chemicals on the menu.

5. During artificial processes like irradiation, non-organic foods lose an ample amount of their nutritional content. Additives and artificial ingredients are also used on the food products to make them last longer. Organic foods do not

lose the nutrients they contain since they are processed naturally.

6. Conventional farming sometimes allows the use of human waste as fertilizers. This is a dangerous practice as this type of waste material can cause sickness and disease. The use of this method is prohibited in organic farming.

7. Industrialized fertilizers have nitrate as its primary ingredient. Nitrates are linked to different types of cancer. Whereas, organic fertilizers have a minimal content of nitrate.

8. Organic farming adheres to the traditional selection of good seeds. Non- organic agriculture resorts to genetically modified seeds that have the ability to grow in varied weather condition but have fewer nutrients.

Chapter 2 - Organic vs. Certified Organic

There are many reasons why you should switch to eating organic foods. However, first you need to know what makes organic food different and how you can determine if the products in your favorite supermarket are indeed organic.

The word "organic" means that it comes from living things and that it still contains carbon. With that definition, it is best to say that organic foods are products that did not undergo any chemical process. They are produced through organic farming and were not processed by using industrial solvent, prohibited pesticides and irradiation-a chemical method that extends food life.

What is the difference between organic and certified organic? The term "organic" is applied to foods that are produced through organic farming but not necessarily have undergone the certification administered by the United States Department of Agriculture through the National Organic Program (NOP). Certified organic is a label to trust because this means that the product was able to meet the standards and requirements set by the NOP.

There are two categories of USDA Seal. First is the 100% Organic USDA Seal, then the Organic USDA Seal. Products that are awarded with the 100% organic seal must have used 100% of the Department of Agriculture's requirement and did not use any non-organic ingredients in processing, packing and handling of the goods. The organic label is attached to products that have at least 95% organic ingredients requirement and 5% ingredients that are allowed by the National Organic Program.

There is a strict law covering the implementation and use of NOP's organic labels. Mislabeling of products is subject to a fine not exceeding $11,000. Producers find a hundred and one ways to make their products appear like organic even if they are not certified by the United States accrediting body.

So how do you know that the product you are buying is organic? The product must have a genuine

USDA seal for it to be considered certified organic. There are many food labels that may confuse you and even make you believe that the food is organic. However, these are not official seals from USDA so you must be keen in buying these products.

Let us talk about them in detail so you would not be misled by these logos:

1. LOCALLY GROWN. This seal means that it was grown and produced in the local region or nearby farms. Although, it doesn't mean that if a product is grown locally, it not sprayed by synthetic pesticides.

2. NATURAL/ NATURAL FLAVORS. This term is a buy-in strategy. Consumers upon seeing this sign will think of the connotation of the word "natural" that it is safe and healthy.

3. FREE RANGE. This label is usually affixed on meat products. This means that animals are allowed to go outdoors and are not kept in a congested cage. However, this is not a guarantee that they are raised without artificial feeds and antibiotics.

4. HORMONE FREE. This is often applied to dairy products. This statement is not true since all animals

have hormones. A more trusted label would be "free from artificial hormones".

5. NON-GMO. All GMO products are not organic, but not all non-GMO foods are grown or produced organically.

6. ADDED/FORTIFIED WITH VITAMINS. This means that nutritional values are added to the food. This is a misleading label since consumers would always connect the word "nutritious" to being healthy. However, it does not give you the details on the sources of these vitamins and does not tell you if such vitamins are synthetic or organic.

7. GRASS FED. It makes you visualize that the cows are allowed to have a free space where they practice appropriate grass diet. Do not be misled with this term, as it does not guarantee that the animal was not supplemented with non-organic feeds.

8. FARM-RAISED. The word "farm" connotes a healthy environment for poultry and livestock. It tells you about the setting or the place where the animals are raised. It does not tell you anything about their diet, and if they are treated with vaccines and other medications.

9. PASTURED. The animals are given free space to walk around and give an image that they eat grass since they are in a pastured land. However, there is no assurance that they were not given antibiotics.

10. SUGAR FREE. This food label often means one thing- they did not add white or brown sugar. Instead, an alternative sweetener is used which is usually a GMO.

11. MADE WITH ORGANIC INGREDIENTS. The phrase "made with" does not make the whole thing organic.

12. ANTIBIOTIC FREE. This label is attached to meat products. Antibiotics are not only the things that make a food non-organic. This is not a guarantee that they were not treated with growth hormones.

13. VEGETARIAN DIET. This food label has almost the same meaning with grass fed. This is an assurance that the animals are fed with the appropriate foods but not a guarantee that it was not given appetite enhancers or any supplement.

Understanding these labels is very important when purchasing products. However, there are products that do not bear the USDA official seal but they are truly organic. These are the products that are produced by farmers who chose not to be certified because of the high cost of the certification process even if their goods are actually organic. So a consumer needs to discover if the food is organic through his own research, relying on the information given by the grower. For your peace of mind, go for the products with the USDA seal or buy products from your trusted local farmer.

Chapter 3 - Why Choose Organic Foods?

Healthy food choices are a vital and the initial step in gaining a happy life lived in a safe environment. What you eat at breakfast and what you serve during dinner would define the quality of your life and would affect the life of other people and the condition of nature. There are many good reasons why you should switch to an organic diet.

1. Organic food contains more nutrients. Vegetables that are packed with fertilizers grow quickly, giving them minimal time in developing nutrients. A farming soil that is free from chemicals and

commercialized fertilizers is favorable to the good quality of crops and vegetables. For example, strawberries that are grown using the organic method contain more antioxidants and ascorbic acid compared to strawberries produced by conventional farming. Organic fruits contain a higher level of iron, magnesium protein and antioxidants.

2. It is free from harmful pesticides and other dangerous ingredients. The absence of these chemicals would mean a stronger immune system; this will boost your white cells to protect you against illnesses and sustain your energy.

3. Organic foods will help you save time and money. These foods may seem expensive at first but if will look at a larger perspective, you will realize that it is actually cheaper. Since you will be guarded against diseases you do not have to worry about future hospital bills or having that monthly check up.

4. It will promote a healthier environment. If you patronize organic products, majority of farmers will transition to organic farming. As a result, there will be lesser use of fertilizers and chemical products, which causes several environmental catastrophes. The absence of commercial fertilizers will promote soil fertility, and no pesticide residues would mean cleaner air. Insects and other organisms are allowed

to live in their natural habitat, thus maintaining the balance in the ecosystem. Ecological processes like natural decomposition will not be disrupted and will serve as an organic fertilizer. Organic farming also prevents the increase if carbon dioxide in the atmosphere. Carbon is trapped in the soil preventing it from contributing to the existing amount of CO_2 in the air. A healthy habit offers a healthy living to all organisms that dwell in it.

5. Foods without pesticide residue will help you enjoy a good night sleep every day. You do not have to worry about the side effects that you can get from the

hazardous chemicals used in industrial farming; one such adverse health effect is difficulty sleeping.

6. Organic foods taste a lot better than conventionally farmed ones. Fresh fruits always taste better and give you that good feeling compared to junk foods that make you feel groggy and weary after eating. An organic roasted beef has richer flavor and texture than the ones injected with growth hormones.

7. It is safe for children and infants. They are more vulnerable to illnesses when exposed to chemicals found in non-organic foods. If you do not like the idea of feeding your baby with vegetables laced with

dangerous chemicals then you should only buy organic produce.

8. Organic foods will make you feel guilt-free. You will enjoy eating everything in your plate because you know that it is safe and good for your health. So you have less worries and a lot of peace of mind.

9. Eating organic foods will help local farmers grow their business.

10. Organic milk contains more omega-3 that is proven to deliver good effects to the heart.

11. Buying and eating organic produce will help minimize the gases present in the atmosphere. Buying foods from the local farmers market would mean preventing those delivery trucks from emitting carbon dioxide because they do not have to transport the goods from distant farms.

Chapter 4 – The Disadvantages of Going Organic

Everything has its own boon and bane. The disadvantages of organic foods however, are very few and will not cause any harm to your health.

1. Organic foods are difficult to find. In an age of Science and Innovation it is hard to find a supermarket that offers a wide selection of organic products. Also, the production rate of organic farming is lower compared to the yield of growers who use commercial fertilizers and pesticides. Having your own organic garden would be a good solution.

2. There are few foods to choose from. Unlike GMO's that can grow in any kind of climate, fruits and vegetables follow a season. Weather conditions affect their growth. That is why it will be hard for you to find a fresh lettuce during the winter because it cannot survive in a very cold temperature.

3. If we are going to talk about the price alone, organic foods are more expensive than commercialized products. This is because the production of these foods requires high cost since they are not using artificial ingredients. Plus, growers

pay a big amount in the USDA Certification and maintaining a certified organic status.

There are plenty of ways to cut the cost of buying organic foods. First is to go to your local farmers market. This is a great place to find fresh, cheaper fruits and vegetables. They are direct sellers so there are no added costs unlike those that are sold in supermarkets. Foods that are sold here are fresh because they came from nearby farms. Compare the prices. Do not just shop at a single store. Explore and find the best deals. Build connection. Visit farms in your area and meet local farmers that you could trust.

Buy fruits and vegetables that are in season. They tend to have lower prices during this time because of an abundant supply. In addition, you are assured that what you are buying is freshly picked from a nearby town and not from another country.

Lastly, you can search for a cooperative in your place that retails organic foods. They usually offer lower prices than the giant supermarkets.

Internet is also a powerful tool than you can use in searching the best deals for organic foods.

4. Organic foods spoil faster since they have no added preservatives. You should eat them the soonest time after you purchased it. The solution is to buy just the right amount of fruits and vegetables that would fit your need.

5. The food production of the organic industry is not proportion to the number of consumers in the planet. The yield is not enough to feed all the people on Earth. More agricultural lands are needed and would mean converting mountains and forests into productive farmlands.

6. The rise of misleading organic labels. Health claims like "all natural" or "no added preservatives" confuses buyers in deciding whether a product is really organic. Many producers try to win customers by putting various labels to foods that are not organic. However if you are a meticulous buyer and you are

detail oriented, this will not be a problem. The secret is to read and analyze each label carefully. Spot the USDA certified organic label and you will be okay.

Chapter 5 - Top Products That You Should Buy Organic

If you are health conscious you must have a list of the foods that you should always buy organic. Buying its conventional counterpart will put your life at risk and your body will be prone to some serious side effects.

1. Beef. The residue of hormones injected to cattle in conventional farming increases the probability of cancer.

2. Apple. The latest research on pesticide contamination awarded the number one spot for apples. It contains the highest level of pesticide.

3. Strawberry. The small bumps outside the fruit absorb the pesticide so well that washing them off is difficult.

4. Grapes. They also contain a high level of pesticides especially the imported variants.

5. Peaches. A huge amount of chemicals are found in peaches skin.

6. Spinach. This green, leafy vegetable accumulates a sufficient amount of pesticides.

7. Sweet bell peppers. Be extra careful in buying fruits that are eaten without peeling off their skins.

8. Nectarines. The pesticide content of conventional nectarines exceeds the allowed percentage.

9. Cucumbers. One of the healthiest fruits that you should include in your diet is cucumber. Always go for the organic version since you will eat it with its skin on.

10. Potatoes. Potatoes grown in a conventional farmland has high risk of pesticide and fertilizer residue content.

11. Tomatoes. Tomatoes carry 30% pesticide level and washing or soaking them in water will not guarantee a decrease in pesticide content.

12. Hot Peppers. Adding that spicy flavor in your dish is a great way to enjoy your meal. Just make sure that you are using the organic pepper that is free from pesticide.

13. Summer Squash. This is the vegetable that was recently added by the Environmental Working Group as one of those vegetables that contains sufficient number of pesticide residue.

14. Kale. Kale is included in the list of products that contains the highest pesticide residue.

15. Collards. This green, leafy favorite has high amount of pesticide residue.

16. Milk. Cows are treated with growth hormones that go to their milk and can be transferred to your body. High amount of this hormone would increase cancer risk.

17. Celery. Their stalk has pores that easily absorbs and retain the pesticides sprayed on it. Bell peppers, spinach, and potatoes that are grown conventionally also have high pesticide content.

There are fruits and vegetables that retain less pesticide because of their thick skins. These are asparagus, avocados, bananas, broccoli, cauliflower, kiwi, mangoes, sweet peas, pineapples, papaya and onions. Other vegetables that have lesser pesticide content are cabbage, cantaloupe, corn, eggplant, grapefruit, and mushrooms. This does not mean that they are safe to eat. Their pesticide content may be lesser however constant and continuous eating of these fruits treated with pesticides is not a good habit. This small amount of chemicals will be accumulated by your body and will still affect your health. It will still be a smart decision to stick with the certified organic fruits and vegetables.

Chapter 6 - Healthiest Fruits and Vegetables

In the previous chapters we talked about the benefits of eating organic habits to your health and to the whole planet. The next thing that is good to know is the list of the healthiest of organic fruits and vegetables that you should never miss in your table.

0. Apples. Apples are very rich in fiber and antioxidant that fights diseases like diarrhea and prevents allergic reactions.

1. Bananas. This fruit has high potassium content that supports metabolism.

2. Blueberries. Blueberries are loaded with manganese that gives you enough energy and boost your metabolism so that you can maintain your good shape.

3. Cantaloupe. It has a large deposit of vitamin A that is responsible for cell regeneration and will make you look younger.

4. Cherries. This fruit contains anthocyanin, an antioxidant that helps lower cholesterol level.

5. Blackberries. Aside from their gem-like appearance this fruit has antioxidants that

may prevent cardiovascular malfunctions and bone problems.

6. Citrus. Lemons and other citrus variants are full of Vitamin C.

7. Cranberries. These tiny berries have big benefits such as fighting urinary-tract infection and giving good cholesterol.

8. Grapes. This fruit is not only famous for being the source of wine but also for its antioxidant content called resveratrol. It releases malic acid that whitens teeth.

9. Grapefruit. Grapefruit is good in keeping a healthy heart.

10. Kiwi. This small fruit is rich in fiber- a major solution to problems concerning digestion.

11. Oranges. Orange is highly recommended to have a strong immune system. It contains the right amount of vitamin c along with other vitamins such as potassium, calcium, fiber and folate.

12. Pomegranate. This beautiful fruit has high anti oxidant content.

13. Plums. Plums have chlorogenic acid that may eliminate tendencies of depression.

14. Avocados. This fruit promotes the increase of good cholesterol in your body and lessen bad cholesterol. It is also good for the heart because it contains lycopene.

15. Papayas. Papayas contain Vitamins C that is good for your immune system as well as Vitamins A and E that are great antioxidants.

16. Tomatoes. Lycopene is the major vitamin content of tomatoes. They also contain fiber and Vitamin C.

17. Raspberries. If you are suffering from digestion problems, eating raspberries is the answer. This fruit is very high in fiber and will give you good digestion.

18. Squash. This is known for its high beta-carotene, which is good for the eyes and helps lower high blood pressure with the help of potassium.

19. Watermelon. Like tomatoes, watermelon also has high level of lycopene. In fact, it has more lycopene compared to the rest of the fruits.

20.   Pineapple. This yellow delight contains a

digestive enzyme so having it

On your plate would mean no worries about

digestion.

21.Onions. Onions have the most number of

antioxidants and best for people suffering

from osteoporosis because of its GPCS

content that prevents the rapid loss of

calcium. This vegetable with a pungent odor

can also help fight heart problems because of

its high level of folate and Vitamin C.

22. Corn. Organic corn contains an antioxidant called lutein that is essential in having healthy and good eyesight especially for adults.

23. Broccoli. Beta-carotene, Vitamin C, and folate are the vitamins that are present in broccoli.

24. Carrots. This is a good source of nutrients that will help you get that glowing skin, healthy eyesight and shiny hair.

25. Eggplant. Eggplants contain a compound named nasunin that is healthy for brain cells.

26.   Brussel sprouts. This green delight contains Vitamin C, fiber, omega 3 fatty acids, potassium and B vitamins. This is especially recommended to pregnant women.

27.   Spinach. This green vegetable has almost all the vitamins and nutrients needed for a healthier life.

o. Bell Peppers. Fighting colon, bladder and other kinds of cancer is one important advantage of eating bell peppers.

Chapter 7 - Dangerous Chemicals Used On Non-Organic Food

Non-organic foods are produced using modern techniques. They are processed using chemicals that destroy the quality of food and lessen its nutritional value. By eating organic foods, you are exposing your body to more than three thousand dangerous toxins from a large variety of pesticides to hundreds of heavy metals and harmful set of solvents. The build-up of various chemical residues poses a threat to consumer's health. Here are some of the chemicals used in non-organic food production and their known effects.

1. Estrogen- cows that are raised in the conventional way are normally given estrogen so that they will be fat and will look healthy. Estrogen may cause cancer and other diseases like infertility and genital malformations. Since the purpose of estrogen is to promote rapid growth, a person who has a high level of this hormone finds it difficult to lose weight. He has high risk of suffering from obesity. So instead of losing some extra pounds, you will lose that abs and curves.

2. Prolactin- this is a growth hormone injected to lactating cows to increase milk production. Growth hormones increase cancer risk and prolactin targets

the nervous system that often leads to depression and tumors.

3. Antibiotics- studies on milk produced in a conventional manner are claimed to have an abundant amount of antibiotics that kills the good bacteria in our system thus, weakens your immune system. Antibiotics in dairy products give birth to a new generation of bacteria, which are resistant to present antibiotics. They are sometimes called super bugs for their powerful ability to survive. This means that your body will need higher dosage of medicine to fight the infections caused by these bacteria. One of these high-resistance bacteria that already caused a number of deaths is Escherichia coli. This is a

substance in conventional cattle feeds that may cause vomiting and diarrhea. Even if our stomach releases gastric acid to get rid of food-borne pathogens, E coli has very high resistance to acid.

4. Saturated fats- non-organic foods contain a big amount of saturated fats and sodium that is detrimental to your well-being. The bad cholesterol scientifically known as low-density lipoprotein (LPP) is formed when the body has a high level of saturated fats. Suffering from diabetes and heart problems are also one of the known side effects.

5. Glufosinate- is a chemical used in sugar and cooking oil that causes serious birth defects.

6. Chlopyrifos and malathion- these are the common ingredients in pesticides that are detrimental to IQ development.

7. Glyphospate- this is a herbicide used in non-organic crops that contain a large amount of harmful toxins. When mixed with other chemicals, glyphospate can cause simple to severe health conditions like memory loss, concentration difficulty, depression, miscarriage, genital abnormalities, and impotence and if exposed during pregnancy stage will lead to severe birth defects such as autism, malformation and nerve damage.

8. Arsenic- non-organic fruits and vegetables show traces of arsenic and other harmful metals. These heavy metals are used as ingredients to some industrial fertilizers and absorbed by the soil and eventually by the crops planted on the soil. Crop rotation is not a practice in the modern method. As a result, farm soil is not given the opportunity to regain its fertility. Heavy metals are stored in the soil for a long time and exposure to this chemical weakens and even destroys nerve functions resulting to lower IQ.

9. Hydrogenated fats- these fats are the primary cause of most cardiovascular diseases and are linked to heart attacks.

10. Insulin- non-organic meats are injected with an insulin-like substance that may cause acne.

11. Additives- these are flavor enhancers added to foods to improve their taste or enhance their texture and appearance. This ingredient is attributed to diseases such as asthma, ADHD, heart problems and cancer. It will take time for some diseases to be noticed, so you have to be careful of the kind of foods that you eat today.

12. GMO- this is a product of genetic engineering wherein experts remove or add a gene in the DNA of a plant or an animal so that they can survive under varied environmental and weather condition. Although the effects of Genetically Modified Organisms to human health are not yet discovered, these organisms are found to be unsafe for animals. Recent studies reveal that some GMOs when given to a set of animals have caused genital defects to their off springs. So you have to be extra careful in buying these products. If it is not safe for animals, then there is a big probability that it is dangerous for human consumption. Furthermore, one active ingredient that is being used in the engineering process is glyphosate,

which carries a high level of toxins responsible for reproductive problems, endocrine disruption, and cancer.

13. Irradiation- non-organic foods undergo the process of irradiation for longer shelf life. This chemical process reduces the level of vitamins in foods. Vitamins A, E and B are reduced from 5-80%. Irradiation kills the good bacteria and destroys the digestive enzymes resulting to slow metabolism.

14. Carcinogenic pesticides- farmers who have direct exposure to pesticides and insecticides are more likely to suffer from various deficiencies such as abnormal

sperm count and diseases concerning their reproductive organ. Non-organic foods also pose high chances of food poisoning because of the chemical residue left in farmlands. This is possible especially for root crops like potatoes and carrots.

Eating non-organic foods does not only affect you health but also the condition of the environment. The use of fertilizers causes soil erosion and pollution. Harmful fertilizers kill beneficial microorganisms like earthworms that keep the soil fertile. The harmful chemicals in herbicides hurt the bees that are essential to pollination. Particles of insecticides and herbicides mix with the air that contributes to global warming. Residue absorbed by the ground surface contaminates the water and aquatic life. The various agrichemicals used in non-organic farming are slowly turning this green planet into an environment that is not safe to all forms of life.

Conclusion

Eating foods that will help support local farmers, and promote animal welfare, a healthy environment and a healthier you is the greatest decision that one will ever make. It is more than just a choice. It is a responsibility because as humans we have a commitment to maintain the natural order of the planet where we live the best way we can.

More so, we have to value our body and live a good life. Everyone would agree on the idea that life is short. Do not take chances on making it even shorter. A diet with organic fruits and vegetables will give you the physical strength, emotional vitality and a positive outlook in dealing with everyday life.

The benefits of organic foods that you serve from breakfast to snacks and dinner cannot be summarized in few pages. Let us just recall the most important advantages. Eating organic foods will save you from suffering from diseases with famous and unfamiliar names. It will also help the small farm owners to grow their businesses, be an advocate of clean air, clean water and healthy soil, and protect the environment from the ravages of agricultural advancement.

Isn't it amazing that by just taking care of your own health, you also contribute to the wellness of other people, the rest of the organisms living in this planet and the future generation? Most importantly, you are saving Earth from the severe, harmful impact of a world that has more faith in the conventional method rather than living the organic way.

The destiny of your health and nature depends on what you eat. Start with a bite of a red, certified organic apple or a sip of fresh milk from organic cows and be an evidence of the endless good things offered by organic food habit.

Printed in Great Britain
by Amazon